FOUR SEASONS POETRY BOOKS

SUMMER

COMPILED BY JENNIFER WILSON

ILLUSTRATED BY GRAHAM COOPER

Macdonald Children's Books

Contents

Early Summer *by Norman MacCaig* 4
The Headless Gardener *by Ian Serraillier* 5
Beetle *by Hugh Finn* 6
Some One *by Walter de la Mare* 7
Shed in Space *by Gareth Owen* 8
Mary and her Kitten *by Eleanor Farjeon* 10
A Small Dragon *by Brian Patten* 11
Evening *by P.B. Shelley* 12
The Bat *by Theodore Roethke* 13
Lapwings *by Laurence Smith* 14
Starling on a Green Lawn *by Norman MacCaig* 15
A Heavy Cart Rumbles *by Kuroyanagi Shoha* 16
Man Carrying Bale *by Harold Munro* 17
The Beach *by W. Hart-Smith* 18
The Sea *by R.S. Thomas* 19
Beaulieu River *by Andrew Young* 20
Fishing Song *by Judith Nicholls* 21
Sunflower *by Judith Nicholls* 22
Throw the Ball *by Edwin Thumboo* 23
The Owl and the Astronaut *by Gareth Owen* 24
Moonlight *by P.J. Chaudhury* 25
The Face of the Dragonfly *by Chisoku* 26
Considering the Snail *by Thom Gunn* 27
Mole *by Alan Brownjohn* 28
Andromeda *by Judith Nicholls* 29
Spraying Sheep *by Norman MacCaig* 30
Puddle Splashing *by Frank Flynn* 31

Introduction

Have you ever played a game in which you match the heads, bodies and legs of different animals or people to make a new creature? The results can be most surprising! You can do something similar with words. Whoever heard of foam rubber clouds, a garden rolling up its sleeves, a starling like a mad glove, the sea's knuckles that it uses to pummel you or a quicksilver flock of sheep? But if you have played with little beads of mercury, or quicksilver which is its more interesting name, and gathered them into one blob to run together through a narrow space and then let them separate again into little balls you will know exactly what the poet means by a quicksilver flock of sheep.

When words are used like that, so that they do not mean exactly what they usually mean, we call them metaphors. Poets can use metaphors to say some surprising things. Look out for words that are playing this game.

Summer is a time to be out of doors and these poems take you outside by day and at night.

Jennifer Wilson

Early Summer

The garden rolls its sleeves up, sweats
And labours in the fiery sun
To heave a flower into the air, and
Unclench a million fists of green.

Birds tip their sacks of sound – the morning's
Lettered like a calendar
With April growing like corn in the ground
And May hung yellow in the air.

The water in the gutters clucks
With light and flies into the sun.
Shadows crowd into doorways. Walls
Expand, forgetting to be stone.

And windows all are nests on fire;
And a million phoenixes now make
Arabia of these roofs and dart
From trees of incense-bearing smoke.

Norman MacCaig

The Headless Gardener

A gardener, Tobias Baird,
Sent his head to be repaired;
He thought, as nothing much was wrong,
He wouldn't be without it long.

Ten years he's weeded path and plot,
A headless gardener, God wot,
Always hoping (hope is vain)
To see his noddle back again.

Don't pity him for his distress –
He never sent up his address.

Ian Serraillier

Beetle

A beetle caught my eye, one day,
Beside the path;
There, with his head buried deep in a daisy centre,
Pigging and bolting it – great, scented, yellow mouthfuls –
With the space he had already eaten
Blackened around him;
There he gorged, standing on his ridiculous gluttonous head,
With his hard, thin legs
Straight up in the forgotten air,
And his head deep in a dim, succulent heaven.

Hugh Finn

Some One

Some one came knocking
    At my wee small door;
Some one came knocking,
    I'm sure – sure – sure;
I listened, I opened,
    I looked to left and right,
But nought there was a-stirring
    In the still dark night;
Only the busy beetle
    Tap-tapping in the wall,
Only from the forest
    The screech-owl's call,
Only the cricket whistling
    While the dewdrops fall,
So I know not who came knocking,
    At all, at all, at all.

Walter de la Mare

Shed in Space

My Grandad Lewis
On my mother's side
Had two ambitions.
One was to take first prize
For shallots at the village show
And the second
Was to be a space commander.
Every Tuesday
After I'd got their messages,
He'd lead me with a wink
To his garden shed
And there, amongst the linseed
And the sacks of peat and horse manure
He'd light his pipe
And settle in his deck chair.
His old eyes on the blue and distant
That no one else could see,
He'd ask,
'Are we A O.K. for lift off?'
Gripping the handles of the lawn mower
I'd reply:
'A O.K.'
And then
Facing the workbench,
In front of shelves of paint and creosote
And racks of glistening chisels.

He'd talk to Mission Control.
'Five-Four-Three-Two-One-Zero –
We have lift off.
This is Grandad Lewis talking,
Do you read me?
Britain's first space shed
is rising majestically into orbit
From its launch pad
In the allotments
In Lakey Lane.'

And so we'd fly,
Through timeless afternoons
Till tea time came,
Amongst the planets
And mysterious suns,
While the world
Receded like a dream:
Grandad never won
That prize for shallots,
But as the captain
Of an intergalactic shed
There was no one to touch him.

Gareth Owen

Mary and her Kitten

The Kitten's in the Dairy!
Where's our Mary?
She isn't in the Kitchen,
She isn't at her Stitching,
She isn't at the Weeding,
The Brewing, or the Kneading!
Mary's in the Garden, walking in a Dream,
Mary's got her Fancies, and the Kitten's got the Cream.

Eleanor Farjeon

A Small Dragon

I've found a small dragon in the woodshed.
Think it must have come from deep inside a forest
because it's damp and green and leaves
are still reflecting in its eyes.

I fed it on many things, tried grass,
the roots of stars, hazel-nut and dandelion,
but it stared up at me as if to say, I need
foods you can't provide.

It made a nest among the coal,
not unlike a bird's but larger,
it is out of place here
and is quite silent.

If you believed in it I would come
hurrying to your house to let you share my wonder,
but I want instead to see
if you yourself will pass this way.

Brian Patten

Evening

The sun is set; the swallows are asleep;
The bats are flitting fast in the grey air;
The slow soft toads out of damp corners creep,
And evening's breath, wandering here and there
Over the quivering surface of the stream,
Wakes not one ripple from its summer dream.

There is no dew on the dry grass tonight,
Nor damp within the shadow of the trees;
The wind is intermitting, dry, and light;
And in the inconstant motion of the breeze
The dust and straws are driven up and down,
And whirled about the pavement of the town.

P.B. Shelley
from Evening

The Bat

By day the bat is cousin to the mouse.
He likes the attic of an aging house.

His fingers make a hat about his head.
His pulse beat is so slow we think him dead.

He loops in crazy figures half the night
Among the trees that face the corner light.

But when he brushes up against a screen,
We are afraid of what our eyes have seen:

For something is amiss or out of place
When mice with wings can wear a human face.

Theodore Roethke

Lapwings

Here come the squealing
clowns
riding the wind
Baggy wings
trip, flap, flip
out of the sky
over the foam rubber clouds
slap in the face of the
sun.
Black and white sleeves
cartwheel over the trees
and fall
and peel out of a roll
Wolf-whistle
and land light on their feet
swank and bow.

Laurence Smith

Starling on a Green Lawn

He makes such a business of going somewhere
he's like a hopping with a bird in it.

The somewhere's an any place, which he recognises at once.
His track is zig – zag zig zag – zag.

He angles himself to the sun and his blackness
becomes something fallen from a stained-glass window.

He's a guy King, a guy Prince, though his only royal habit
is to walk with his hands clasped behind his back.

Now he's flown up like a mad glove on to a fence post.
He squinnies at the world and draws a cork from a bottle.

Norman MacCaig

A Heavy Cart Rumbles

A heavy cart rumbles
And from the grass
Flutters a butterfly.

Kuroyanagi Shoha

Man Carrying Bale

The tough hand closes gently on the load;
Out of the mind, a voice
Calls 'Lift' and the arms, remembering well their work,
Lengthen and pause for help.
Then a slow ripple flows along the body,
While all the muscles call to one another,
'Lift!' and the bulging bale
Floats like a butterfly in June.

Harold Munro

The Beach

The beach is a quarter of golden fruit,
a soft ripe melon
Sliced to a half-moon curve,
having a thick green rind
of jungle growth;
and the sea devours it
with its sharp,
sharp white teeth.

W. Hart-Smith

The Sea

They wash their hands in it.
The salt turns to soap
In their hands. Wearing it
At their wrists, they make bracelets
Of it; it runs in beads
On their jackets. A child's
Plaything? It has hard whips
That it cracks, and knuckles
To pummel you. It scrubs
And scours; it chews rocks
To sand; its embraces
Leave you without breath. Mostly
It is a stomach, where bones,
Wrecks, continents are digested.

R.S. Thomas

Beaulieu River

Largest of Forest snakes, by heath and scrog
It stretches in its blue sky-borrowed coat,
For while its tail trails in a cotton bog
It grips with foaming mouth the Solent's throat.

Andrew Young

Fishing Song

Ragworm, lugworm, mackerel, maggot,
Grey pike lurking, still as steel.
Cast my rod in the deep dark stream
With a nugget of bread for a silver bream.
Caught an eel.

Ragworm, lugworm, mackerel, maggot,
Number Ten hook and I'm waiting still.
A carp would be good or a spiny perch,
A golden rudd or a red-finned roach?
It's an eel.

Ragworm, lugworm, mackerel, maggot,
Something's biting, wind up the reel!
Is it a pike or a roach or a rudd?
A hunting gudgeon from the river bed?
Just – an eel.

Judith Nicholls

Sunflower

guards my south wall,
a private sun.
Floodlights the whole garden,
warms tardy flowerbeds into life
in leafy July.

She turns to face the sun – we're told;
I know it's wrong.
Really the sun chases my Inca goddess,
jealous of rival gold.

Judith Nicholls

Throw the Ball

Let's throw the ball at the sun,
Make it laugh and sigh,
See it hide and smile and run,
Then fall from the evening sky.

Let's throw the ball at the moon,
And watch it falling down,
Then catch it with a silver spoon
In the middle of the town.

Edwin Thumboo

The Owl and the Astronaut

The owl and the astronaut
Sailed through space
In their intergalactic ship
They kept hunger at bay
With three pills a day
And drank through a protein drip.
The owl dreamed of mince
And slices of quince
And remarked how life had gone flat;
'It may be all right
To fly faster than light
But I preferred the boat and the cat.'

Gareth Owen

Moonlight

I saw moonlight lying on the ground,
I stooped and touched the ground with my hand.
And found it was common earth,
Dust was in my palm.

P.J. Chaudhury

The Face of the Dragonfly

The face of the dragonfly
Is practically nothing
But eyes.

Chisoku

Considering the Snail

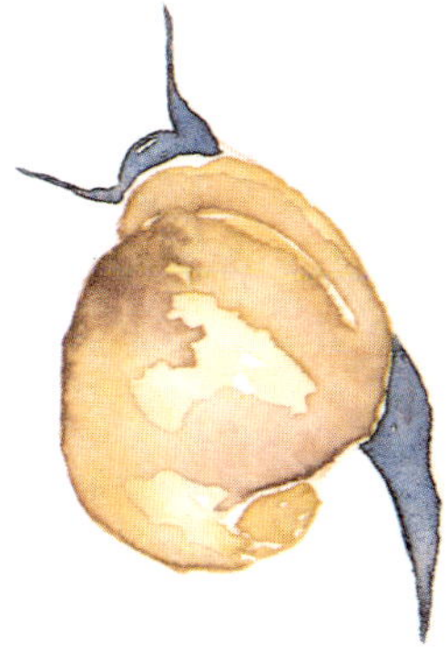

The snail pushes through a green
night, for the grass is heavy
with water and meets over
the bright path he makes, where rain
has darkened the earth's dark. He
moves in a wood of desire,

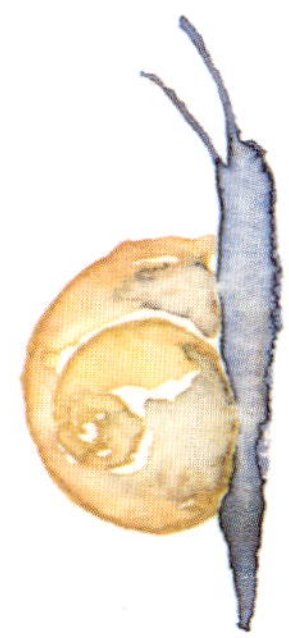

pale antlers barely stirring
as he hunts. I cannot tell
what power is at work, drenched there
with purpose, knowing nothing.
What is a snail's fury? All
I think is that if later

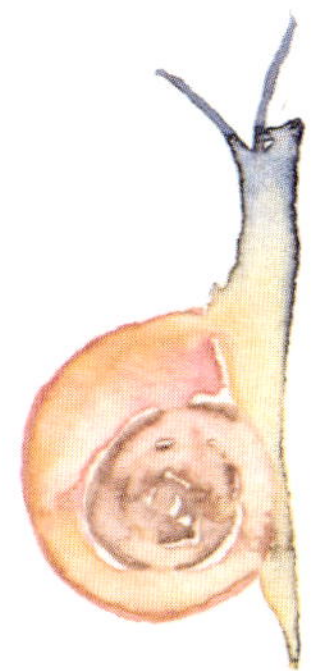

I parted the blades above
the tunnel and saw the thin
trail of broken white across
litter, I would never have
imagined the slow passion
to that deliberate progress.

Thom Gunn

Mole

To have to be a mole?

It is like, in a way,
being a little car driven
in the very dark,
owned
by these endless-
ly tunnelling paws and small
eyes that are good, only,
for the under-ground.

What can you know of me, this
warm black engine of
busying velvet?

Soft mounds of new, pale
earth like finely-flaked ash
tell you just about where

my country is, but
do you ever see
me?

Alan Brownjohn

Andromeda

On a mole-black night when the stars are bright
And the cloud-veiled moon is high,
If you search near the wings of Pegasus
You can see her in the sky.

Chained fast to a rock, she waits her fate
As the great sea-monster's prey;
As she hides in fear she can hear the hiss
Of Cetus on his way.

But wait, it's the swish of Pegasus' wings
With Perseus riding high!
On a mole-black night with the stars in flight
You can see them ride away.

Judith Nicholls

Spraying Sheep

Old tufts of wool lie on the grass.
The clipping's over. But once again
The small quicksilver flock come pouring
Down from the hill towards the pen.

Dogs coax them to the roofless steading.
They bunch, plunge forward, one by one.
When half's outside and half within, they
Make a white hourglass in the sun.

The dogs run on the ruined walls,
Swinging their tongues, their minds all sheep.
The zinc bath winks, the stirrup pump
Guzzles the primrose one foot deep.

Then out they come, bounding high over
Nothing at all, and ramble on
The shining grass – not quicksilver
But golden fleeces, every one.

Norman MacCaig

Puddle Splashing

I'm fed up
with dry sunny days
because I've got this pair
of brilliant, bright, brand-new
yellow wellingtons
that shine like a new car
and come right up to my knee.
The next time it rains
I'm going puddle splashing
with my mate Jake.
Jumping from puddle to puddle
we'll make tidal waves,
or damming gutters with our boots
we'll turn streets into lakes,
while our laughter shakes raindrops
off the leaves of watching trees.

Frank Flynn

Acknowledgements

Culford Books wish to thank the following for their kind permission to use their material:

'Mole' Alan Brownjohn from BROWNJOHN'S BEASTS Macmillan, London & Basingstoke. 'Moonlight' P. J. Chaudhury from SELECTED POEMS Writers Workshop (Calcutta, 1978). 'The Face of the Dragonfly' Chisoku from A HISTORY OF HAIKU The Hokuseido Press trans. R. H. Blyth. 'Some One' Walter de la Mare by permission of the Literary Trustees of Walter de la Mare and The Society of Authors as their representatives. 'Mary and her Kitten' Eleanor Farjeon from INVITATION TO A MOUSE Hodder & Stoughton. 'Beetle' Hugh Finn from NEW POEMS English Centre of International P.E.N./Huchinson 1954. 'Puddle Splashing' Frank Flynn from THE CANDY-FLOSS TREE: poems by Gerda Mayer, Frank Flynn, and Norman Nicholson Oxford University Press. 'Considering the Snail' Thom Gunn from MY SAD CAPTAINS Faber & Faber. 'The Beach' William Hart-Smith from his book SELECTED POEMS 1936-1984, reprinted with the permission of Angus & Robertson Publishers. Copyright © William Hart-Smith 1985. 'Early Summer', 'Starling on a Green Lawn', 'Sheep Spraying' Norman MacCaig from COLLECTED POEMS by Norman MacCaig Chatto & Windus Ltd. 'Fishing Song', 'Sunflower', 'Andromeda' Judith Nicholls from MAGIC MIRROR Faber & Faber Ltd. 'Shed in Space', 'The Owl and the Astronaut' Gareth Owen from SONG OF THE CITY William Collins Sons & Co Ltd. 'A Small Dragon' Brian Patten from NOTES TO THE HURRYING MAN Allen & Unwin (Publishers) Ltd. 'The Bat' Theodore Roethke from THE COLLECTED POEMS OF THEODORE ROETHKE Faber & Faber Ltd. 'The Headless Gardener' © 1946 Ian Serraillier, and Oxford University Press. 'A Heavy Cart Rumbles' Kuroyanagi Shoha from THE PENGUIN BOOK OF JAPANESE POETRY translated by Geoffrey Bownas and Anthony Thwaite (The Penguin Poets, 1964), p 118, copyright © Geoffrey Bownas and Anthony Thwaite, 1964 reproduced by permission of Penguin Books Ltd. 'Lapwings' Laurence Smith from CATCH THE LIGHT: poems by Laurence Smith, Gregory Harrison and Vernon Scannell (1982) Oxford University Press. 'The Sea' R. S. Thomas from YOUNG AND OLD Chatto & Windus Ltd. 'Throw the Ball' Edwin Thumboo from CHILD'S DELIGHT Federal Publications © Pte Ltd, Singapore. 'Beaulieu River' Andrew Young from THE POETICAL WORKS OF ANDREW YOUNG Martin Secker & Warburg Ltd.

A MACDONALD CHILDREN'S BOOK

First published in Great Britain in 1987 by
Macdonald & Company (Publishers) Ltd
This edition Macdonald Children's Books
Simon & Schuster International Group
Reprinted 1989

Conceived, edited, designed and produced by Culford Books,
Sunningwell House, Sunningwell, Abingdon,
Oxfordshire OX13 6RD
Edited by Penelope Miller
Designed by Judith Allan
Photoset by Lantern Graphics Ltd

Printed and bound in Great Britain by
BPCC Paulton Books Limited

Macdonald Children's Books
Simon & Schuster International Group
Wolsey House, Wolsey Road,
Hemel Hempstead HP2 4SS

British Library Cataloguing in Publication Data

Summer. —— (Four seasons poetry).
1. Summer —— Juvenile poetry 2. Children's poetry, English
I. Wilson, Jennifer II. Cooper, Graham
III. Series
821'.008'033 PZ8.3

ISBN 0-7500-0040-6